Mind Over Matter

Anastasia Frangoulis

Mind Over Matter © 2023 Anastasia Frangoulis

All rights reserved.

No part of this publication may be reproduced, stored in a retrieval system, or transmitted, in any form or by any means, electronic, mechanical, photocopying, recording or otherwise, without the prior written permission of the presenters.

Anastasia Frangoulis asserts the moral right to be identified as author of this work.

Presentation by *BookLeaf Publishing*

Web: www.bookleafpub.com

E-mail: info@bookleafpub.com

ISBN: 9789357441704

First edition 2023

Mind Over Matter

The mind is a battle we are trying to fight but
sometimes we cannot see the light.
The mind is an obstacle we face but it is absurd
that this is the case.
The mind is what controls us but our thoughts
beholds us.

The Mind

2

The mind is not seen
It is complex and can be mean
The panic , the despair , the torture our mind can
bring.
One day we hope to see light at the end of the
tunnel and darkness

Love + Mind

Her mind was all over the place with different thoughts and mental thinking with negative emotions.
It was like someone stole her soul and made it have power over her by creating a monster within.
It was then she realised - her mind and brain was controlling her. Nobody else but her was to blame.

How the Mind works

4

Mental health is not a destination. It is a path where we lead to create better and stronger memories. To become the better self and the better version of us. Sometimes we have to go through the worst to get the best.

The Battle

5

She loved and she always loved. She loved so
much that she lost herself and her heart within.
She thought there was nothing left but to love.
Then one day she became numb , because she
was so hurt and drowned in the pain that nothing
or nobody could save her.

The Mind and Self Love

6

Be happy , healthy and most of all have self love. Is it easier said than done? No. It should be done. Self love comes from the heart, mind and soul and nobody should break that. You should make , create self love within.

Loving someone

I have loved and I have always loved but does not mean that love is good for us and our minds. It does not mean it is healthy for our souls. It can be damaging and harmful. Love can hurt deeply like a knife but loving the wrong person can hurt more.

What is love?

I never knew what love was till I met you. I always thought to myself "if I don't love you then I don't know what love is" till this day. I still believe that. Till this day I still love you with all my heart and soul. Nothing or anyone can ever change the way I feel. No matter how many obstacles we had to go through and the pain in me was caused . I still love you. From the moment we met . I will love you till the day I die.

Storm

Whatever storm you face there will always be light at the end of the tunnel. We have to go through the worst to get the good. It is not love that causes us pain, it's loving the wrong person.

A positive Mind

The mind controls our thoughts which leads to emotions. We need to learn to control our mind and have positive thoughts. If we can control our mind then we can control our life.

Definition of Who I Am

Sometimes I do not know what to do or say and I lose control and I lose myself in negative thoughts. I somehow learn to get up and overcome it because my negativity doesn't define who I am.

Love Yourself Indefinitely

12

Learn to love yourself because nobody can love you if you don't love yourself. Learn to be content and have peace within.
It does not come naturally so you need to work on yourself everyday and it will eventually follow. It takes time and practise.

No Place Like Home

13

There is no place like home
Home is in your arms
Home is in your eyes
Home is in your hands
Home is in your heart
Home is where I feel safe

Everything I Do

Everything I do and everything I see reminds me
of you.
What I say and express is true.
You have shown me what love is
And how love is supposed to be.
And I felt free.

My Mind

15

My mind runs wild
My mind runs free
But when I am with you I am full of glee.
My mind is a rollercoaster of emotion
It feels like an ocean.
My mind explores new possibilities but it has so
many responsibilities.

The Mind Does Matter

Mind over matter
All it does is chatter
Mind over matter
It does scatter
Mind over matter
The mind does matter

It is a saying

17

Mind over matter is a saying that we always
express but sometimes it is used less. Mind over
matter is what we need to remember but it is
now December.
Mind Over Matter can be controlling but it is
never ending.

The Mind & Self Love

18

Self love comes from the heart within but it also
part of the mind.
The mind can control our self love and
emotions. We need to learn to control our mind
to have the self love within our hearts and
minds.

www.ingramcontent.com/pod-product-compliance
Lightning Source LLC
LaVergne TN
LVHW050313200726

843509LV00015B/3295